MIGHTY MACHINES

A LEGO® ADVENTURE IN THE REAL WORLD

> All aboard for a monster machine adventure!

■ SCHOLASTIC

New York Toronto London Auckland
Sydney Mexico City New Delhi Hong Kong

Welcome, LEGO fans!

LEGO® minifigures show you the world in a unique non-fiction programme.

This reader is part of a programme of LEGO® non-fiction books, with something for all the family, at every age and stage. LEGO non-fiction books have amazing facts, beautiful real-world photos, and minifigures everywhere, leading the fun and discovery.

To find out more about the books in the programme, visit www.scholastic.co.uk

Levelled readers from Scholastic are designed to support your child's efforts to learn how to read at every age and stage.

Gold level books include some sophisticated and challenging vocabulary. They introduce word play and more complex text layout. Some Gold level books have short chapters to challenge and encourage reading stamina.

BUILD IT!

Check out the epic building ideas when you see me.

If you see a word in **bold**, you can find out what it means on page 31.

Hey, can I have a lift? I need to get to the end of this book!

Look around you. Machines help out everywhere! Giant diggers lift tonnes of dirt. Long trains pull carriages full of people. Rockets blast into space.

Mighty machines are super-strong - just like me!

I wonder how much the biggest digger bucket can hold?

It's big enough to scoop me! I'm off!

Start your engines.
Let's go!

BUILD IT!
Build your own
mighty machine.
Will it have wheels
or wings?

8905 8905

635

BNSF

8905

Make way!
Longest road train
coming through!

Let's build a road! Call in the digger. The digger has an arm called a boom. It has a bucket on the end. The sharp teeth **scoop** out earth.

The biggest digger in the world could hold 4,000 footballs.

Awesome! I'll kick them in. GOAL!

Octan

The biggest diggers are as heavy as 400 cars!

BUILD IT!
Build a digger. How many LEGO bricks can you scoop up?

The biggest dump truck tyre is as tall as 100 minifigures!

The dumper truck brings earth and rocks to make the road. It may hold about 25 tonnes of dirt.

Hmm, this is tough work. I'd rather have a big scoop of ice cream.

That's as heavy as 5 big elephants! It tips out the earth ready for the bulldozers.

Call in the bulldozer! The bulldozer uses a big **blade** to push the dirt and rocks. It makes everything flat. A super dozer has a blade that is as wide as 462 minifigures!

Our road needs to go through that old building.

Stand back! I'm going to blow the building up.

Oops. Wrong one! Quick, where's the bulldozer?

The bulldozer has giant tracks to help it move. I'd better make tracks!

Bring in the steamroller!
It may weigh 20 tonnes.
It smoothes **tarmac**
on to the road.
Now the road is built.
Let's drive!

Help! I don't want to become a flatbread!

Chill out, man. It's only travelling at 1.99 miles per hour (3.2 km/h)!

BUILD IT!

Build cars, motorbikes and trucks for your road. Create a huge traffic jam!

Concrete is good for building. The concrete mixer has a barrel that turns round and round. It mixes cement, rock and water to make concrete. When the concrete is poured out, it hardens.

Ooh, I'm sinking into this concrete.

Careful! Concrete turns hard really quickly.

Yikes! I'm not going to stick around to find out!

How do you build a super-tall building? A crane can lift what you need! The tallest crane can lift things up to 70 **storeys** high.

BUILD IT!

Build a crane with a super-long arm. Remember to build a strong base for it!

I said pick up the bar, not my car!

Some machines are used to carry things. Honk honk! The road train is on its way. It can pull up to 100 **trailers**! Road trains are the longest trucks in the world.

Oh no, I think we've got a puncture.

Are you kidding me? There are 100s of tyres to check.

Found it, finally! Yawn. That's tired me out...

BUILD IT!

Build a road train. How many trailers will it have?

Some trucks can carry other heavy things. A car transporter carries between 5 and 10 cars. The cars drive on and off **ramps**.

BUILD IT!

Build a car transporter to carry cars all around your house.

Heeeeave!

Cars weigh about 2 tonnes each! That's heavy.

All aboard! The **cargo** ship travels all over the world. It holds more than 2,000 big boxes. One ship may be as long as 13 blue whales!

Check this out! The biggest cargo ship can hold more than 745 million bananas!

Toot Toot! Trains pull carriages full of people.

Can you tell me where the toilet is please?

I'm afraid it's at the other end of the train.

Argh! This train is soooo long!

The longest trains have 44 carriages. One train in Japan travels at 375 miles per hour (603 km/h)!

Tickets, please! Hurry up, this train is super-speedy!

Zoom! The Airbus jet flies at 540 miles per hour (869 km/h). It holds more than 500 people.

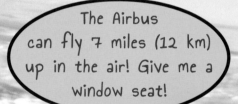

The Airbus can fly 7 miles (12 km) up in the air! Give me a window seat!

It is the biggest plane in the world. It has two levels!

BUILD IT!

Build an awesome plane and take your minifigures on holiday.

AIRBUS A380-800

3, 2, 1,
blast off! The
Soyuz rocket blasts
into space. It moves at
230 metres per second.
It takes astronauts to
a **space station**.

Look, aliens!
But how did
they get there?

We've got company.
Let's get the
flying saucer.

Hello there!
Anyone up for
a space race?

It's the mightiest
machine of all!

BUILD IT!
Build a rocket
to carry LEGO
bricks into space.
Perfect for
building
your
space
station!

Build a LEGO® construction site!

Mighty machines love to work. What will you build today?

Mighty machine words

blade
The broad, flat part of a machine that pushes the material to be moved.

cargo
Something that is carried from one place to another by a vehicle.

concrete
A hard, strong material that is used for building.

ramp
A slope that joins two surfaces of different heights.

scoop
To dig out.

space station
A large spacecraft in which people live, to do research and experiments.

storey
A part of a building where all the rooms are on the same level – also called a "floor".

tarmac
A black material that is used for making roads.

trailer
A wagon that carries heavy loads and is pulled by another vehicle.

This axe is no good. Bring in the mighty machines!

Shhh!

It's good to learn some mighty words!

Index

A
Airbus 26
astronauts 28

B
barrel 14
blade 10, 31
boom 6
bucket 4, 6
building 16
bulldozer 9, 10, 11

C
car transporter 20, 21
cargo 22, 31
carriages (train) 24, 25
cars 7, 11, 13, 20, 21
cement 14
concrete 14, 15, 31
construction site 30
crane 16, 17

D
digger 4, 6, 7
dumper truck 8

EFG
engine 5

HIJKLM
mixer 14
motorbike 13

NOP
plane 27

QR
ramp 20, 31
road 6, 8, 11, 12
road train 5, 18, 19
rocket 4, 28, 29

S
ship 22
Soyuz rocket 28
space 4, 28
space station 28, 29, 31
steamroller 12
storey 16, 31

T
tarmac 12, 31
trailer 18, 31
train 4, 24, 25
truck 8, 13, 18, 20
tyre 8, 19

UVWXYZ
wheels 5
wings 5

Credits

For the LEGO Group: Peter Moorby *Licensing Coordinator*; Heidi K. Jensen *Licensing Manager*;

Photos ©: cover main: Blaize Pascall/Alamy Images; cover top left: goce/iStockphoto; cover top right: Juanan Barros Moreno/Shutterstock, Inc.; cover, back cover tire tracks: Yevgen Solovyov/123RF; 1 cloudy sky and throughout: Pop Nukoonrat/Dreamstime; 1 main: Josie Elias/Getty Images; 2 center left: i-Stockr/iStockphoto; 2-3 bottom background: Bryljaev/Dreamstime; 4-5 train: John Kirk/iStockphoto; 6-7 main: gece33/iStockphoto; 7 top right: JamesYetMingAu-Photography/iStockphoto; 8-9 top: Maksym Dragunov/iStockphoto; 8 center left: Alasdair Thomson/iStockphoto; 10-11 main: Blaize Pascall/Alamy Images; 10-11 tape: Arcadia_dreamstime/Dreamstime; 11 center right: nulinukas/Shutterstock, Inc.; 12-13 background: mycola/iStockphoto; 12-13 main: Yudesign/Dreamstime; 13 bottom right: Molotok007/Dreamstime; 14-15: Krzyzak/Alamy Images; 16-17 top background: roman023/iStockphoto; 16 top: Lalocracio/iStockphoto; 17 top right: Various-Everythings/Shutterstock, Inc.; 18-19: Josie Elias/Getty Images; 20-21: Taina Sohlman/iStockphoto; 22-23: Peter Titmuss/Alamy Images; 24 bottom left: VCG/Getty Images; 24-25 main: Vincent St. Thomas/Shutterstock, Inc.; 26-27 background: Brian Kinney/Shutterstock, Inc.; 27 right: Artyom Anikeev/Shutterstock, Inc.; 28-29 background: olegkalina/iStockphoto; 28-29 main: NASA/Joel Kowsky/Alamy Images; 30-31 sky: Matthew Collingwood/Dreamstime; 30-31 bottom: Ciezkitemat/Dreamstime; 30 center left: keantian/Shutterstock, Inc.; 31 top left: gece33/iStockphoto.

All LEGO illustrations by Paul Lee and Sean Wang

Here are the LEGO bricks, ready for your next build!

Scholastic Children's Books,
Euston House,
24 Eversholt Street,
London NW1 1DB, UK

A division of Scholastic Ltd
London ~ New York ~ Toronto ~ Sydney ~ Auckland
Mexico City ~ New Delhi ~ Hong Kong
This book was first published in the US in 2017 by Scholastic Inc.
Published in the UK by Scholastic Ltd, 2017

ISBN 978 1407 17235 4